zendoodle coloring

Creative Sensations

Other great books in the series

zendoodle coloring

Calming Swirls

Enchanting Gardens

Inspiring Zendalas

Creative Sensations

Hypnotic Patterns to Color and Display

illustrations by

Julia Snegireva

ST. MARTIN'S GRIFFIN

NEW YORK

www.stmartins.com

ISBN 978-1-250-08648-8 (trade paperback)

St. Martin's Griffin books may be purchased for educational, business, or promotional
use. For information on bulk purchases, please contact the Macmillan Corporate and
Premium Sales Department at 1-800-221-7945, extension 5442, or write to
specialmarkets@macmillan.com.

First Edition: August 2015

10 9 8 7 6 5 4 3 2 1